365

ways to be INSPIRED

365 WAYS TO BE INSPIRED

An Hachette UK Company
www.hachette.co.uk

Vie Books, an imprint of Summersdale Publishers Ltd
Part of Octopus Publishing Group Limited
Carmelite House
50 Victoria Embankment
LONDON
EC4Y 0DZ
UK

www.summersdale.com

Printed and bound in the Czech Republic

ISBN: 978-1-78685-767-5

Substantial discounts on bulk quantities of Summersdale books are available to corporations, professional associations and other organisations. For details contact general enquiries: telephone: +44 (0) 1243 771107 or email: enquiries@summersdale.com.

365

vie · *ways to be* INSPIRED

Start a journal and make a conscious effort to write in it every day, either as soon as you wake up, when you get home or just before you go to bed. You could sketch in it, write about your day, list five things that made you smile, or describe your day in a limerick.

2

Find an outdoor activity that you haven't tried before and give it a go – it could be anything, from an art trail to taking surfing lessons.

Join a yoga or t'ai chi class – both will help you to be physically stronger, mentally calmer and more open-minded to the inspiration around you.

4

Prepare a meal using only seasonal produce –
beetroot, kale, turnips and pears are great for
winter, while peppers, courgettes and berries
are all deliciously fresh in the summer.

5

Invent a new word (one that sounds
at least slightly plausible!) and try
to use it as much as possible to
see if other people pick it up.

6

Find a penfriend or online friend in another country,
so you can describe your experiences of living in your
respective cultures and marvel over the similarities
as well as the things that are wildly different.

Take a different route to work, and take special notice of your new surroundings.

Laugh as much as possible today.
Ask everyone you see to tell you their
favourite joke, watch your favourite sitcom,
or go to see a live stand-up show.

9

Revisit a book or movie that held particular significance for you as a child.

Consider one of your daily routines – could it be improved? If so, how?

10

Go into your garden or local park, pick a tree and draw it in as much detail as possible. Make a date to visit the tree in spring, summer, autumn and winter and record how it's changed by drawing it again.

Look up something you have never quite understood,
or have always wanted to know more about.

**Look up a traditional dance and learn
the basic steps using online videos.**

Make your own flavoured oil by lining the bottom of a
sterilized bottle with rosemary or chillies and filling it with heated olive oil.
Leave in a cool, dark and dry place for three months until it's ready to use.

15

Find a local craft class and sign up for a sculpting, woodwork or glass-blowing course – anything that grabs you.

Cut out "must" and "have to" from your vocabulary for the day. Replace them with "I'd love to" or "I can't wait to" – even if it's "I can't wait to do the washing up!"

17

Document your day in photos.

18

Whether it's just the everyday stuff or something special, try to find something beautiful in everything you do, for one day.

19

Make papier mâché models of some common birds, such as robins, wrens and finches, and paint them to display in your home.

20

Sign up to take part in a charity run, walk or skydive later in the year, and start preparing for it now.

21

Have a "no such thing as a stupid idea" journal – one where you can write literally anything that pops into your mind without fear of judgement. If it helps put your mind at rest, you could have this as a password-protected document or app. Make sure you have it with you at all times.

Listen to a genre of music that's out of your usual comfort zone. You could ask a friend for a recommendation or scout out some new music online.

Dig out an old board game (or go hunting for one in a second-hand store) and invite some friends around to play.

Write a haiku about snow.

Buy a beer- or wine-making kit and see if
you can concoct a delicious drop of hooch.
Design your own label for your bottles.

26

Watch your favourite programme on television then, straight away, start writing a sequel to the episode. Even if it's a game show, make it as dramatic as possible.

Buy a colouring book and a pack of crayons. Spend half an hour colouring in and don't worry about staying inside the lines!

27

28

Imagine you have just won the jackpot in the Lottery. Write a dream list of all the things you'd do with your new fortune.

Buy yourself a Rubik's cube – and master it.

Go for a brisk walk for 30 minutes –
your mind will relax and inspiration will come!

31

Listen to a podcast that discusses big issues and write down all the important points that are discussed – consider your stance on each of them.

32

Visit your local church, temple, mosque or synagogue. Even if you are not religious, or belong to a different faith, take the time to appreciate the architecture and the atmosphere of a place of worship.

Buy a magazine or newspaper you would never usually consider and see if it gives you a new perspective on things.

Draw your hand. Put in every line you can see, even if this means it looks more like a ball of string than a hand!

35

Leave your TV, laptop, tablet and mobile phone turned off for a whole afternoon. Spend your time absorbing the sights, smells and sounds of your neighbourhood.

36

Volunteer a few hours of your time to a charity shop or homeless shelter, and strike up friendly conversations with all the people you meet.

Close your eyes and imagine yourself waking up in five years' time. What does your room look like? Are you alone or with someone? What are you wearing? Use these images to spur you on to attain your goals.

Teach yourself to touch-type. It will make writing your first novel that much faster!

39

Think about something you take for granted every day –
consider how you might do things differently without it.

40

Find an art print, photo or poster that really
inspires you, frame it yourself and put it in
a place where you will see it often.

41

Read your favourite poem aloud. You absorb words
in a different way when you hear them spoken.

Make a playlist for someone, full of all the music you think they will love but haven't discovered yet. Really put thought into the content and the order of the songs.

Create a quirky sculpture out of spare bits and pieces you have lying around – make it as elaborate as possible.

Embrace your passions. Whatever it is you feel really strongly about, or whatever your talent – share it with others today. Spread your knowledge and enthusiasm.

Write a poem about a famous historical figure you admire.

46

Download an art-related app on your phone – try "Craftsy", "Artsy", "Brushes" or "Typendium". Every time you're tempted to open a social media app on your phone, open this one up first!

47

Plant a tree in memory of someone that was close to you. If you don't have anywhere to plant a tree, why not name a star after them instead (there are ways to do this online)?

Introduce yourself to a neighbour –
preferably bearing baked goods!

Stop what you are doing and take a half-hour nap.
Your mind continues to work subconsciously while you sleep, so
when you wake up, you may have an unexpected "Eureka!" moment.

Read the poem "The Summer Day" by Mary Oliver.

Draw up some basic plans for redecorating a room in your house. Make a list of ideal décor and draw up a floor plan. Once you have your ideas together, look into how to get the work done and take the first steps to transforming your living space.

52

Choose an album that's been reviewed in this week's paper and download it, then spend an hour or two really listening to it, in order.

53

Create your own style by designing and making a T-shirt print. Use card to create a template and apply the design to a blank shirt using fabric paint.

54

Fill a whole page of a notebook with doodles. Draw whatever comes to mind.

Visit your nearest live music venue and buy
tickets to see whoever is playing this week.

Buy some fresh flowers for your home –
they'll add colour and life to the room.

57

Go down to your local train station, town square or park and spend an hour people-watching.

58

Buy a pumpkin-carving kit and try your hand at a more intricate design than a simple scary face.

59

Write as many sentences as you can to do with the colour black.

Take a bus ride to somewhere you've never been before (just make sure you check the timetable, so you can get back!).

60

61

Call a family member that you don't speak to very often, and find out what they've been up to.

Go outside and smell the fresh air. Take deep breaths and really notice everything you can about its smell. Now come back inside and try to describe it – in prose, poem or painting.

62

Give meditation a try – it can be as simple as sitting comfortably in peaceful surroundings and being aware of your breathing, in and out, in an effort to clear your mind of all thoughts. Aim for ten minutes to start with.

64

Ask a musical friend to give you a lesson on their instrument. Aim to learn at least one simple song.

65

Search for the most shocking, outrageous piece of art you can find in a museum of modern art (most have online galleries you can look through, if you can't get to one in person).

Play "Just a Minute" – try to talk for 60 seconds on one topic without hesitating or repeating any words except the subject words.

Find some tranquillity by enhancing the peacefulness of your bedroom. Invest in some blackout blinds, ear plugs, new sheets, a luxurious mattress or anything else that will make each night's sleep perfect.

Invent a new sandwich using your favourite foods. Once you've created your culinary masterpiece, invite some friends over and make it for them.

Plan and book a weekend in the great outdoors.

Find a tasty vegan recipe and cook
it for your friends or family.

Design your own stained-glass window and construct it using cellophane and craft paper.

71

72

Write out, by hand, your favourite passage from a great book, or something you've read today that strikes you as powerful. Using a pen and paper will help you connect with the message.

73

Create a cartoon strip to illustrate your day.

Practise contour drawing: sit in front of a mirror and draw your face, without looking down at the piece of paper. It might not look like much but it'll be fun!

Organize a book-swap club. Everybody brings along a number of unwanted books, and you can take away as many as you came with!

Wake up ten minutes earlier than usual and stretch every major muscle in your body. If you can, find a set of stretches to follow. It'll set you up for a great day.

77

Set goals to complete over the coming week: complete one sketch per day, write 1,000 words per day, cook with one new ingredient per day – whatever takes your fancy.

Invent and draw a new type of vehicle.

78

79

Create a feature wall in a room of your house that is overdue for redecoration. Choose one strong, bold colour or wallpaper that really expresses your personality. For the renters among us, you can find temporary and removable wallpapers online.

80

Prepare a special dessert to give yourself a well-deserved treat.

81

Read *The Seven Habits of Highly Effective People* by Stephen Covey, or *How to Win Friends and Influence People* by Dale Carnegie. Even better – read both! Put their points into action.

82

Cut out a picture of the lower part of a face (preferably with amusing features) and stick to the bottom of a friend's mug. When they drink from it, everyone will laugh – and they won't know why!

83

Organize a visit to your nearest brewery and try one of the unique tipples on offer there.

84

Start a page of a notebook to write down funny words that amuse you: "flibbertigibbet" or "nincompoop", for example. Try to top up the list at least once a week.

85

Volunteer to walk a friend's dog, or to walk the dogs at your local shelter. Being around animals naturally relieves stress and centres the mind.

86

Listen to the sound of rain on your umbrella, and make up a tune to complement it.

87

Feel inspired the next time it rains: splash paint onto thick watercolour paper, then hold it outside briefly for the elements to work their magic. Use the colourful paper as the background for an art project.

88

Take arty photos of some of your favourite objects and put them together in a scrapbook.

89

Find a news story that interests you. Try to imagine you are the central person in the story and write an entry of their diary which covers the newsworthy event.

90

Plant tomato or salad-leaf seeds in pots to keep on your windowsill. In a few weeks you'll be creating some delicious salads!

Decorate the first page of a blank notebook with poems, pictures or doodles. Post it to a friend to fill in page two then return it to you. Keep going until the book is full.

91

92

Write a letter to someone without using the words "I", "me" or "my".

Buy a pack of sculpting clay at your local art or craft shop, and see what you can make.

Think of a piece of clothing or an outfit that makes you feel good about yourself. Why not get more of the same style? Make room in your wardrobe by donating the clothes you never wear to charity.

Greet everyone you meet today in continental fashion by kissing them on each cheek.

Find your own positive affirmation and practise repeating it to yourself whenever you feel at a loss. "I am strong and confident" or "I am happy and successful" work well!

Energize yourself with a brisk swim – outdoors if possible!

98

Collect some stones or shells from a park or beach, and paint them in beautiful colours.

Write a sonnet to the person you care about most in the world. Take a first line from a sonnet by William Shakespeare or Elizabeth Barrett Browning to get you started.

99

100

Make a journey in a way you're not used to – take the bus to work, cycle to the pub, take a taxi to a friend's house.

101

Write an amusing or poignant message on the dirty window of a car or van.

102

Play the word association game with yourself: write down your starting word and see where you end up.

103

Work on picking up a new (good) habit or dropping
an old (bad) one – for 21 days. This is the length
of time it takes to form or lose many habits.

104

Make a list of all the different jobs you've had. Write
about them – your experiences, memories, whether you enjoyed them.
Then write about your dream job and compare the accounts.

105

A spring clean is always a good idea –
a clear space is fertile ground for new ideas.

106

Go to a nature reserve to try to pick up ideas about what you could do to help the birds, bees and other animals in your area.

107

Dance! For no real reason, wherever you are. Pretend you're in a scene in a musical. You could sing, too, if you like.

Take a sketchbook on the train and see if you can sketch a scene or object just from a fleeting glance.

Get a group of friends to each write a two-minute stand-up sketch, then throw a comedy night in your front room to laugh the night away!

Make a list of everything you love in life: your favourite songs, great friends, good food, the smell of just-cut grass...

Rearrange or redecorate your home workspace – or if you don't have one, create one. It can be anything from a comfy bean bag to a library and bureau – but make sure it suits you.

112

Practise your hobby for five minutes every day for a month. See how much you can get done with regular short, intense bursts of activity.

113

Take advantage of asparagus season (it's short!). Buy in bulk and make asparagus soup, asparagus and caramelized onion tarts, grilled asparagus with goat's cheese...

114

Practise the "Memory Palace" technique (the art of remembering things through mental images) to improve your recall.

115

If you make a mistake while creating or performing, try reacting positively instead of berating yourself. Say to yourself "nice try!" or "I've learned not to do X" and start again.

116

Compliment everybody you meet on one thing you genuinely like about them.

Get an impromptu haircut – it can revitalize your outlook on life, as well as how you feel about yourself.

Start a nature diary and record all of the plants and animals you come across while out walking (if you don't know the names, take photos and look them up afterwards or sketch them instead).

Try the old art of brass rubbing.

120

Even if you'll never go through
with it, design your dream tattoo.

121

Buy yourself a hat – the quirkier the better.

122

Jazz up your kitchen by painting old and faded plates,
teapots, biscuit tins or even cupboard doors with crazy patterns.

123

Plan a cultural trip to Europe – a weekend in Paris, five days in Barcelona, a city-hopping tour of the Balkans – travelling by high-speed train.

124

Educate yourself on a religion, country or culture you know little about.

125

Arrange a debate night with some close friends. Bring out the refreshments and discuss a current controversial topic. Do some research first and keep it civil – but make it interesting!

126

Have a go at making your own seasonal decorations out of odds and ends you have in the house – you can decorate the house for any reason, not just for a birthday or Christmas.

127

Take the first step towards something you've always
wanted to do, but that has daunted you in the past.

128

First thing in the morning, write down five
reasons why today will be great. Keep the list with
you and refer to it throughout the day.

129

Go to a poetry reading or open-mic night. Even better, volunteer to read a poem or perform one of your own songs.

130

Take your exercise gear to work and go for a brisk jog on your lunch break. Don't forget the baby wipes, if your workplace doesn't have showers!

131

Write about your favourite memory of one of your parents or family members.

132

Find the music festival nearest to where you live and get tickets!

Spend all day actively listening to the people you talk to. If you ask somebody how they are, let them say more than "fine".

133

134

Create the wildest outfit you can to wear to work.
If your boss won't take offence at skin-tight leopard
print and fluorescent socks, go for it!

135

Keep a notebook and pen next to your bed and
record your dreams as soon as you wake up. Get a
dream dictionary to interpret their meanings.

136

Take up a hobby inspired by the Victorian era – cultivate
some interestingly shaped facial hair, ride a penny-farthing,
have a go at embroidery or candle-wax statuette making.

137

Watch a foreign movie with the subtitles on.

138

Visit your local swimming pool and splash and play as if you were five again. Even better if the pool has waterslides!

139

Volunteer to help at your local summer fair.

140

Revisit the psychedelic sixties by searching online and listening to some far-out music from that decade – groovy, man!

141

Burn some incense and sit quietly enjoying the aroma. Let your thoughts stray to wherever they want to go.

142

Visit a museum dedicated to something you have no current interest in – you may be pleasantly surprised.

143

Make your own crossword using an online puzzle generator. Make the clues personal and send it to friends and family.

144

Write a letter to someone you've always admired but have never been in contact with.

Visit a special outdoor spot to watch the sun come up – even better if you can do it on the longest day of the year.

Find an online community for people in your profession – you'll meet people with similar aims and outlooks as you, and your stories are bound to inspire each other and give you fresh perspectives. Arrange or attend a social networking event and meet some new people.

147

Select one of your favourite stories and create one or more new characters in the "universe" – draw or write them into being.

148

Write down a great memory that made you smile or a joke that made you laugh. Fold up the paper and hide it in the pocket of a jacket you don't always wear to be found in months to come.

149

Design your own coat of arms, flag or emblem – make it so it reflects your values and personality.

150

Listen to a new song or an old favourite on repeat, thinking each time about a different aspect of it – the rhythm, the lyrics or the melody.

Scream at the top of your lungs, punch a pillow as hard as you can, and release all your pent-up energy.

151

152

Think up five new metaphors or descriptions
you think nobody will have ever used
before ("This counter is an oryx's horn
full of pirouetting shadows").

153

Take an old coat or jacket and decorate it
with badges and patches. If you don't have any
badges or patches, start collecting some now!

154

Find yourself a "positivity trigger". This can be anything which has good connotations for you – a key ring, a photo, or even a small stone or shell you can keep in your pocket. Take it out any time you need a boost.

155

Lie on the grass and watch the sky.
See the patterns in the clouds.

156

Organize a motivational event at work – how about an afternoon of Office Olympics?

Visit a local arts cafe
and enjoy soaking up the
creative atmosphere as
you sip your coffee.

Think about someone
in your life you respect
and admire – what could
you learn from them?

Go back in time and seek
some ancient wisdom from the
Buddhist text *The Dhammapada:
The Path of Perfection.*

160

Create an "inspiration board" at home. Pin up and attach things that you find inspiring – anything at all from cards to labels to leaves!

161

Find out where the highest natural point in your area is and (as long as it's not dangerous!) visit it to experience the view.

Find a recipe that gets your mouth watering,
then get down to the supermarket, pick up
the ingredients and start cooking!

163

Hire a fancy-dress costume and
wear it out with your friends.

164

Design your own board game – why not invite
some friends around to play it with you?

165

Go along to a protest march and soak up some
of the passion and emotion. Alternatively,
why not start a petition of your own?

Go to the insect house at your local zoo, or natural history museum, and watch the way that leafcutter ants work together to achieve their goal.

166

167

Spend an evening at a restaurant you've never been to before – and order something you wouldn't usually eat.

Try to write a song using only three notes.

168

169

Create a piece of "cut-up" writing. Collect single pages from different newspapers, magazines and other publications; cut each page into several pieces and then mix and match the sections to create new sentences.

170

Draw yourself as a character from your favourite book.

171

Decorate your desk at work or at home with pictures of people or places that inspire you, calm you or motivate you.

172

Try your hand at a pub game – darts, dominoes, cribbage, bar billiards. If you find you enjoy it, search for a local team or league nearby.

173

Recreate a scene from a favourite movie or novel – swinging around lamp posts in the pouring rain or hijacking the mic on a parade float to sing "Twist and Shout".

Get down to your local park or playing field
for some outdoor sporting fun!

Gaze out across a pond or stream and watch the way the fish,
dragonflies and water boatmen affect the water's surface.

Spend a few minutes slowly crafting the perfect
sentence. It could be about the emotions you're feeling
right now, your favourite season, the taste of your morning
coffee... anything, but make each word count.

77

Be a tourist in your own town: go to the Tourist Information office, pick up leaflets, and go sightseeing!

Go to the beach and dig your toes into the sand. Listen to the waves on the shore. Think about the colour of the sea, the taste of the salty air. Think of one word which perfectly sums up what your senses are experiencing.

78

Design a comic book cover that imagines you and your friends as superheroes.

179

180

Go to a car boot sale or charity shop and buy a cheap guitar or keyboard. Even if you have never played before, make up a song.

Sleep outside under the open sky.

181

Make a fruit salad using no less than
eight different fruits – try adding a
dash of your favourite fruit-flavoured
liqueur to give it a bit of oomph!

183

Write a message to yourself and put it in a bottle and bury it. Dig it up after five years (or when you move) and reminisce.

184

Throw a winter garden party. Fill your back garden with chairs, cushions and blankets and a fire pit or chiminea, and serve warming food and drinks.

185

Wear 1920s-style clothes to work.

186

Try learning a new language. Download an app or buy a "teach yourself" book, and commit to learning five new words or phrases per day.

187

Make your own ice lollies using only natural ingredients – or have a go at making ice cream if you're feeling adventurous.

188

Find a meditation workshop event near you and give it a try.

189

Find an indoor ski slope and give it a go!

190

Visit a bookshop and select a book at random – buy it and read it from cover to cover.

191

Organize a water-pistol war with friends –
don't forget balloons for water bombs!

192

Think of one thing that would make a big
change in your work life and drop it in your
suggestion box. If your workplace doesn't
have one, suggest that they get one!

193

With time and distance comes perspective: think of something you have abandoned in recent months – an idea or a project – and try to think of ways to make it succeed.

194

Buy a yo-yo and aim to learn at least five tricks.

195

Watch an outdoor performance – there are often classical concerts or Shakespeare performances in the summer, and you might get lucky at other times of the year if you keep an eye out!

196

Go boating – on a canal, river, lake or at the seaside, whatever you fancy.

Walk or cycle slowly down a road and imagine who lives in each house. Create a dramatic story for each one – a secret addiction, a love affair or some literal skeletons in closets!

197

Do one good deed today.

198

Think about your home and how you could make it more environmentally friendly – whether by simply unplugging all your electronic appliances when they're not in use or investing in solar panels.

199

Find a piece of art, literature or music that is at least 1,000 years old, and create its modern counterpart.

200

Try going through the weekend without checking the time – ignore your clock/watch/phone and simply act on impulse.

202

Start a family tree using photos of your relatives –
or, if you're short on photos, why not draw them?

203

Do something you haven't done since you were
a child – climb a tree, play with a ball, go on a
bike ride to the park – and try to recapture the
silliness and joy you would have felt as a child.

204

Create some quirky and original
bookends out of found objects.

205

Look outside and count how many different shades and colours you can see. Think of the perfect word to describe each tone: olive, pistachio, lawn green, jungle green, mint, chartreuse.

Draw an object you look at every day, such as a peanut butter jar, your handbag or your overflowing chest of drawers. Draw every detail, taking your time.

206

Go outside and photograph at least five different animals.

207

208

Read as many poems as you can today. Try to find one poem which perfectly summarizes your mood right now.

Go outside at night and lie on the ground (somewhere comfy!) looking up at the stars. Imagine life on distant planets – who might be looking back at us right this second?

209

210

Pick a country you'd like to live in for a year,
if you could choose anywhere, and research it.

211

Make a Green Man for your garden out of clay or a
collection of natural materials such as twigs and leaves.
If you don't have a garden, make one for your local park.

212

Switch on the radio and make up alternative
lyrics to the songs that come on.

213

Read a classic novel that you never
thought you'd get round to reading.

214

Create a piece of Banksy-style street art using a
stencil and spray paint on a large canvas.

215

Organize a regular movie night with friends, where you watch each of your favourite movies in turn (one each night).

216

Recreate the "blind dining" experience at home – eat in the dark, so that your other senses are heightened.

217

Immerse yourself in a virtual fantasy world by signing up for an online roleplaying game.

218

Look for a new recipe involving chocolate and cook two batches – one to give away and one to keep!

219

Volunteer to help tend the grounds at your local park or communal garden.

220

Close your eyes and breathe as slowly as possible.
Become aware of all the things you can feel: the
weight of your body on your chair, your hair against
your forehead, a slight breeze through a window.

221

Print some photos of yourself and your friends and have a doodle session. Use a white Sharpie to draw over them with silly hairstyles, funny accessories and new landscapes.

222

Flick through today's paper and cut out words or phrases that strike you as interesting. Arrange your words and phrases to make a statement or poem.

223

Play – hide-and-seek, hopscotch, tag...

224

Go to see the original of your favourite painting in an art gallery, if you can, to see how different it looks in reality as opposed to as a print.

225

Consider these words from the Dalai Lama: "We can never obtain peace in the outer world until we make peace with ourselves."

Take a duvet day or unscheduled holiday and spend the day doing absolutely nothing at all!

226

227

Make or design a piece of jewellery for someone you love.

Use aural stimuli to help you with your work. Try listening to sound effects such as a rough, crashing sea or birds twittering (you can find them online) before you get going.

228

229

Dig out your school yearbook or report book and think about how you have changed – and how you have stayed the same.

230

Try your hand at writing a children's story – you could even add your own illustrations if you feel up to it.

231

Make bunting and use it to decorate your garden or the front of your home.

232

Research the history of your home town.

233

Buy a set of origami paper and
learn how to fold a shape.

Go to a jazz or swing club and soak up the atmosphere.

Experiment with making your own cocktail – think about your favourite alcoholic drink, your favourite fruits and soft drinks and see what you come up with!

Create a scrapbook to document your day – keep your receipts, tickets, wrappers and other bits and pieces you encounter and arrange them together on a page.

237

Design your own typeface (drawn out by hand or using a computer), or choose an unusual one.

238

Read a book set in a country you've never visited.

239

Challenge someone to a game of chess – you can play online if you don't have a board. If you don't know how to play, use today to learn.

Buy frames for your favourite photos and arrange them on one large wall in your home. Or if you have lots of little snapshots, pin them to the biggest cork board you can get your hands on.

241

Go to an online photo-sharing website and find three photos which grab your attention. Next, try to form a story from the photos.

242

Research a company or organisation that interests you. Read their mission statement and learn about their values and ethics.

Try a type of tea that you've never tasted before.

243

244

Get lost. Walk down an unexplored road or path and see where it leads.

Rent a cottage in the countryside, preferably one with a real log fire, and escape there for a night or two with a pile of good books and a bottle of wine.

245

246

Use a voice recorder to record the sounds of your day.

Dance around your front room like nobody's watching.

247

248

Buy a small, plain paper notebook and create a
flip-page animation of something that makes you smile.

249

Read *The Diving Bell and the Butterfly* by Jean-Dominique
Bauby and reflect on the things we take for granted.

Set your music to shuffle and skip to the last line of the third track. Use this line as inspiration for a piece of writing, perhaps as a title or a first line.

Find a food shop you don't usually go to and browse for inspiration – or even better, do your weekly shop there!

Go hunting for apples or edible berries growing wild, and bake a pie or cake with the goods.

Go outside and howl at the full moon.

Revisit the neighbourhood in which you grew up. Take an hour or two to wander around and soak up the memories.

254

255

Fill one side of A4 paper with your argument for something you feel passionately about. Fill the other side with the strongest counter-argument you can think of.

Find a recipe for pumpkin soup, or pumpkin pie, and give it a try.

256

257

Spend the day imagining how life would be if you were really tiny or if everything else had shrunk, à la *Gulliver's Travels.*

258

Draw something with a Sharpie pen – add a design to an old mug, or decorate a plain photo frame, perhaps.

259

Ask a parent to describe the events leading up to and immediately after your birth. Write about it as if you were a fly on the wall.

260

Is there a type of dance you've always admired? Look into classes now.

261

Think of the silliest thing you could do right now. Do it.

262

Revisit an animated cartoon series you enjoyed as a child.

263

Wear something yellow today – it will make you feel happy!

264

Imagine yourself as a cat or a dog –
what kind would you be? Draw or write about it.

265

Try to go a whole day without
saying anything negative.

Go to the top of the highest hill around and watch the magnificent sky turn from day to night.

266

267

Research and construct a "dream machine" for yourself (a home-made flicker lamp which produces silhouettes that stimulate your optical senses).

Try being creative with wool – knit a scarf, a pair of socks or a tea cosy.

268

269

Make a list of the personal values and character traits that are most important to you.

270

Visit your local library and go to a section you'd never think to look at.

271

Write a letter to yourself five years ago, or five years in the future. Tell yourself things you wished you'd known or things you hope to remember.

Light a candle and focus on the movement of the flame and the quality of the light. Allow yourself to just be still and quiet, for as long as you like. Enjoy the silence.

273

Make your own paper using pressed flowers and vegetables.

274

Find a picture you like. Turn it upside down, and try
to copy it. You'll be surprised how differently you look
at things when viewing them from a new angle.

275

Read a novel in a day. Preferably curled up on a sofa with a supply of your favourite hot drink and biscuits.

276

Think about a person in your life who you admire. Visualize their face, think about their attitude and body language and personality, and work out what it is about them that makes them great.

277

Write a story that is exactly 100 words long. Then write a story that is exactly 10 words long.

278

Buy a pack of blank postcards. Doodle, paint or stamp designs on the fronts of all of them, write your favourite inspirational quote on the back, and send them to your favourite people.

279

Download an interesting podcast debate or TED talk and listen to it on your commute. Try to take in as much of the discussion as possible.

Create your own design
for the cover of one of
your favourite albums.

280

281

Buy yourself a set of weights
(even if they are the light ones!)
and commit to doing a certain
number of reps every day.

Think of two words that you suspect
nobody has ever put together
before, such as "crunchy aerobics"
or "salamander pancakes".

282

283

Write down one major change you want to make in your life. See if you can break it down into three smaller, more realistic changes. Now break one of those down even further and make one of those changes today.

284

Cook a meal that includes all of your five-a-day fruit and/or vegetables.

285

Make your own flavoured liqueurs.
You could be as sophisticated – herbs, spices
and wild fruits – or as fun – sweeties, chocolates
and crazy flavour combinations – as you like.

286

Buy a paper and don't put it down until you've solved
the 'challenging' crossword or Sudoku all by yourself.

287

**Listen to a composition by Mozart –
he inspired Albert Einstein, and he may inspire you too!**

288

Get out of a rut: shake up your daily
routine by having lunch in a new spot,
or with a different colleague.

Go to a life-drawing class with a friend.

289

290

Fill an entire A4 sheet with colourful patterns or motifs – make them as simple or as complicated as you like.

Smile at everyone you pass for the day, and notice how it affects the way you feel.

291

292

Watch a classic black-and-white movie and notice
the artistry in the cinematography.

293

Pay a surprise visit to a friend or relative
you haven't seen in a while.

294

Lie down, close your eyes, and visualize every step of a
journey you once made and would like to recall. Relive the sights,
smells and sounds you encountered, and how you felt along the way.

Treat yourself to a long bubble bath, complete
with candles and some relaxing music in the
background. Let your mind wander.

Plan out the screenplay for the movie of your life so far.
Work out which actors will play all the main parts.

297

Go to the ballet or opera – or, if you're already a ballet regular, why not seek out a street-dance performance or something out of your comfort zone?

Make presents for your closest friends or family: a decorated photo frame, a scrapbook of memories, or home-made candles or soaps.

298

299

Make gingerbread and decorate it with snowy-white icing.

Find a cheap last-minute flight online and enjoy an unexpected, but perhaps needed, break.

300

301

Compose a song about the current season –
either a classic to go down in history or a comedy
attempt only fit to be sung to your friends!

302

Pick out an object that you find cheerful
and draw it using wax crayons or coloured
pencils with simple, spontaneous lines.

303

Read a book that's been translated into
your mother tongue from another.

304

Dig out or buy the largest pot or pan you can find and make a sharing dish for all your friends – a paella, stew or chilli are great to get you started.

305

Design your own movie poster – it could be for a made-up movie or one of your all-time favourites.

306

Make mulled wine or sangria, depending on the weather.

307

Sign up for a culinary afternoon – try a workshop on chocolate-making, pasta-making or cocktail-mixing, or a guided walking tour that focuses on one food item: coffee or beer, perhaps?

Attend an event at a local pub or bar that you wouldn't usually go to.

308

Put your change to one side every day for a week and then treat yourself to something on Sunday.

Fill a page of a sketchbook with different styles of shading: smudge pencils or graphite, perfect your cross-hatch, and drag crayons horizontally across the page.

Think of an activity you can share with your family (not something you usually do together) and do your best to convince them all to take part.

312

Review any old cards, letters, pamphlets or programmes you may have kept. Be firm in throwing out the ones you don't want any more and stick the ones you'd like to keep into a scrapbook.

313

Design and make thank-you cards for all the people who have given you gifts recently.

314

Turn to one year ago today in your diary and reflect on what has changed.

315

Attempt to set a world record. It doesn't have to be athletic or extreme – try something fun like "most chocolates eaten in a minute" or "longest daisy chain".

316

Make a piece of art in your back garden using coloured sand and let it blow away.

317

Draw on an unusual canvas, such as
a leaf or a page from an old book.

318

Make a dish that features in one of your favourite
books. Read the description as you eat and be mindful
of the taste, texture, smells and temperature.

Meet with your friends and tackle a problem together, whether it's the crossword, an escape room or even a computer game level. You'll experience different problem-solving techniques which may help you in the future.

320

Find out about any local myths or legends in your town – you could even see if there's a ghost walk nearby you could attend, to hear all the spooky stories.

321

Go outside at night and search for shooting stars and comets, constellations and far-off galaxies. Download a stargazing app and try to name the stars and planets you can see.

322

Rewrite a fairy tale or myth in a modern setting.

Sit on the sofa in your home and close your eyes – what do you notice? Perhaps you tune in to the texture of the sofa or a noise you've not heard before.

Go climbing. It engages your muscles and your problem-solving skills, plus you get to see the world from a different perspective!

Try to do a cartwheel or handstand.

326

Choose an unfamiliar cuisine and eat dishes only from that culture for a week, including breakfast, lunch and dinner.

327

Make a stencil or print using objects around the house such as a sponge or a potato.

328

Think of a type of natural environment you don't visit often, such as marshland, sand dunes, mountain tops or moors, and spend the day there. If you can't get to it in real life, try immersing yourself in the landscape via documentaries, online articles and photos and descriptions in travel books.

329

Make a grown-up goodie bag for your friends to take home with them next time you see them.

330

Start a doodle diary. Instead of writing each day, draw one doodle portraying something that happened or that you enjoyed – even if it's just the weather!

331

Pretend the floor is lava and navigate your way around your home using cushions, tables, etc. Using a space you know well in an unusual way will put you in a new mindset.

Spend time teaching yourself how to construct something practical for your home, such as a small table or a planter.

332

333

Curate a list of independent shops and artists and buy all your presents from them for a year.

Contact one of your parents and arrange to spend the whole day with them and indulge in some of their favourite hobbies.

334

335

Arrange a "lesson" with your creative or practically-skilled friends and spend the afternoon learning from each other. Take it in turns to teach each other the basics of a skill or talent you have. Try to make it so you all have something tangible to take away at the end.

336

Do something different with your lunch break. Meditate, or take a long walk, or even visit a place in the area that you haven't been before.

Try an amateur acting workshop. Even if you don't want to be an actor, you'll learn a lot about exploring and expressing your feelings.

338

Look up a list of unusual jobs from history and imagine what it might be like to work at one.

339

Do some kitchen science, such as trying to mix oil and washing-up liquid or making a volcano with vinegar and baking soda.

340

If a local town or city holds a fringe festival, go to see at least one free show.

341

Download a new podcast that talks about something you're not familiar with; it could be niche history, anecdotes from normal people, deep dives into science or technology or even a work of fiction.

342

Spend today saying "yes" to every opportunity that comes along.

343

Take a photo. Now try redrawing it in different art styles – minimalist, surrealist, abstract expressionist, impressionist or any that take your fancy.

344

Take part in an international drive to create, such as NaNoWriMo (National Novel Writing Month) for writers or Inktober for artists.

345

Make the loudest, weirdest noise you can.

346

If you're getting distracted while working on something creative, try a physical break instead of a mental one: Kurt Vonnegut would do push-ups as part of his writing routine.

347

Go to a bar alone – be open and act confidently. You're bound to meet some interesting characters or even make new friends!

348

Lie flat on the floor and take a photo of what you see.
It's interesting to see the world from a different perspective.

349

Avoid "blank page fear syndrome" by dripping tea,
coffee, ink or paint on the page. The page is now
"spoiled" so your artwork can only make it better!

350

Play a piece of music five different times with
five different emotions in mind: how about anger,
joy, sadness, shyness and playfulness.

Go to your local park and play on the swings or use the zip line (provided no children are using them). You'll give yourself a little rush, for free.

351

352

Pick a theme such as space, dinosaurs or the sea and make a meal inspired by that.

Create a character in your head, and write down everything you can about that person – their interests, how they like to dress, what their deepest fears or secrets are, the celebrities they have crushes on...

353

354

Review your latest creation and give yourself some real talk. What isn't working? What could you have done better? Don't be afraid of constructive criticism – you can only grow if you know where you need to improve.

355

Try a month of inflexibility. Carve out a little time to work at your art and always keep that date with yourself, no matter what you're invited to.

Find three positive things to say about
a famous work that you dislike.

357

Try painting with an unusual body part,
such as your elbow or chin.

358

Go for a walk in the countryside in bare feet.
Splash in rivers and clench grass in your toes
(watch out for animal droppings though!).

359

Invite your friends to partake in a round-robin work;
each person must write a little bit of story, create a bit of art or compose
some music before handing to another friend to add their work.

360

Visit a trampoline activity place and bounce around wildly for half an hour. Let your inner child fly!

Take a road trip (either by car or bike) – with no planned destination. Set off and take whichever route takes your fancy. Let your instincts guide you at each turning or junction and see where you end up! Just make sure you have a way of finding your way home at the end of your adventure.

361

362

Rotate your notebook or sketchbook every time you turn the page.

363

Buy a thimble cabinet and fill it with small, unusual things you find while going about your everyday life. Create a piece of art based on each of those objects – or the cabinet itself.

Create a self-portrait using only unusual materials.

364

Write to three people whose work you admire,
describing how they've inspired you.

If you're interested in finding out more about our books, find us on Facebook at **Summersdale Publishers** and follow us on Twitter at **@Summersdale**.

www.summersdale.com